# THE IRISH FAMINE

First published in 2000 by
Mercier Press
PO Box 5 5 French Church St Cork
Tel: (021) 275040; Fax: (021) 274969; e.mail: books@mercier.ie
16 Hume Street Dublin 2
Tel: (01) 661 5299; Fax: (01) 661 8583; e.mail: books@marino.ie

Trade enquiries to CMD Distribution 55A Spruce Avenue
Stillorgan Industrial Park Blackrock County Dublin
Tel: (01) 294 2556; Fax: (01) 294 2564
e.mail: cmd@columba.ie

A CIP record for this book is available from the British Library.

ISBN 1 85635 299 4
10 9 8 7 6 5 4 3 2 1

Cover design by Penhouse Design
Printed in Ireland by ColourBooks Baldoyle Dublin 13

# THE IRISH FAMINE 1845–52

## EDWARD PURDON

MERCIER PRESS

# CONTENTS

# 1

## DISTRESSFUL COUNTRY

The famine of the 1840s is the great cataclysm of modern Irish history, the apocalyptic event that changed things utterly. It lives with us yet, a nightmare that haunts even after a century and a half, and, as in most recollected nightmares, disbelief aggravates the sense of horror. Stories of the quick being buried in mass graves with the dead, of reusable coffins with sliding bottoms, of families shutting their doors and masking their windows before surrendering themselves to eternity, of crazed mothers eating the flesh of their dead children, of a dying man so weak with hunger that he is unable to bring a piece of bread to his mouth, of thousands of wretched people turned out of their miserable hovels in winter – many to die by the roadside – of a million deaths from starvation and famine diseases, of coffin ships and the bitter irony of many thousands dying of typhus in Grosse Île, the quarantine island in the St Lawrence River, become incomprehensible in the context of modern European 'civilisation'.

The event that reduced the population of the country by a quarter through death and emigration inevitably provided nationalists with the rhetorical certainty of the proof of British wrongs. It was to them the last, unforgivable crime against the nation that had suffered centuries of misrule, exploitation and – to come straight out with the word – enslavement. For many decades afterwards Irishmen (a majority of them in 'exile') could quote a version of the thunderous words of John Mitchel (1815–75): 'The Almighty indeed sent the potato blight but the English sent the Famine' or recite the much-anthologised lines from 'The Famine Year' by Jane Francesca Elgee (c. 1820–90), the mother of Oscar Wilde:

*Weary men, what reap ye? Golden corn for*
*the stranger.*
*What sow ye? Human corpses that wait for*
*the avenger.*
*Fainting forms, hunger-stricken, what see*
*you in the offing?*
*Stately ships to bear our food away, amid the*
*stranger's scoffing.*

This sense of inexplicable injury combines with an understandable urge to comprehend what happened and brings in the further question of whether the disaster could have been prevented or at least made less frightful. At the same time the imp of the perverse that lurks in all Irish psyches wants it never to have happened and hopes for the reassurance that things were not quite as bad as they are reported to have been. Further, a kind of residual guilt about how one's ancestors survived when so many did not makes us look for a kind of exorcism. We need a licence to bury the Great Hunger in the past, with all proper reverence, in contrast to the maimed rites that were the norm for so many Famine funerals.

These are the problems of the interested layman; historians in their different disciplines apply their cliometric techniques to realise the event economically, politically and sociologically. Though truth is absolute and probably unobtainable, these individual perspectives, however different in emphasis, show ever more light. Yet the usual obligation to view the events of the past objectively and not presume to make moral judgements on them somehow breaks down under the pressure of so many emotions, engendered mainly by the difficulties involved in trying to comprehend mid-nineteenth-century attitudes with the eyes of modern confidence.

The reasonable person of today, accustomed to state welfare and the practice of declaring particular regions disaster areas, finds it hard to understand the virtual refusal of the Whig government from 1846 to interfere with the *laissez-faire* ('let do') system of economics, which allowed the export of food from Ireland during the Famine years, and which with hindsight seems to us a recipe for many deaths; or to accept the 'providential' view of the disaster held by many of those in positions of power (Catholic clergy included): the visitation had been sent by a just Creator to remedy the serious social evils of the current Irish situation.

The most excoriated of those who urged these views was Sir Charles Trevelyan (1807–86), the under-secretary at the Treasury, who was the main determiner of the nature of Famine relief. This hard-working, conscientious, devoutly Christian man afterwards stated in the anonymously published *The Irish Crisis* (1848): 'The deep and inveterate root of social evil has been laid bare by a direct stroke of an all-wise and all-merciful Providence.' His monograph was written essentially to defend prevailing economic and socio-religious beliefs. The *laissez-faire* system may have had a rational basis, unexceptionable in times of economic prosperity and perhaps effective as a long-term expedient, but the situation of Ireland in the mid-1840s required emergency measures that needed the repeal of these 'natural' laws.

One underlying reason for the government's unyielding attitude on the Famine was the fact that the British establishment essentially despised a majority of the Irish population. The way the country was run appeared to them almost a profanation of right practice. It seemed quite appropriate that a landlord class that was seen as self-indulgent and prodigal should have tenants who were equally feckless. The western country was reluctantly made part of Great Britain in hugger-mugger by the Act of Union of 1800 but it did not have an equal place at the master's table. This union was maintained as much for psychological reasons as for any advantage it offered to the commonwealth. The loss of the American colonies had left its mark and no further fraying of the fabric of the steadily growing British Empire would be permitted.

Only the counties of the north-east, where the undoubted acumen of the Ulster–Scot was giving Ireland its sole taste of the Industrial Revolution and where the lately prosperous market town of Belfast was being turned into a classical Victorian city, were a matter of pride. There in July 1849, while the Famine still raged and emigration had reached haemorrhage levels, leading members of the council, accompanied by a military band, sailed through the new

Victoria Channel, which allowed large vessels to dock virtually in the town centre. This successful piece of engineering prepared the way for the necessary imports of raw material which would make Belfast a city of heavy industry and lay the keel, so to speak, for its famous shipyards.

The rich lands of south Antrim, the Lagan valley, most of Down and Armagh and the Foyle Basin (almost entirely owned by Protestants), with their diversified agriculture, neat modern farms and different practice in land tenure, made the region seem a model of what a worthy economy should be. Mainland investment was concentrated there, with all British governments taking their view of Ireland from the loyal but generally unaristocratic Protestants. By then, too, Henry Cooke (1788–1868) had all but expunged radicalism from his Presbyterian followers and had established friendly relations with the Church of Ireland, a rapprochement made relatively easy by that church's instinctively 'low' norms. Ulster loyalists became just that – solid Tory–Unionist and ready at times of crisis to form a united front against papism. There was also a certain mercantile buoyancy in such ports as Waterford and Derry; Cork maintained its old primacy and Dublin, as the capital, could be sure of a limited prosperity. The situation in the country as a whole was vastly different, however.

Agriculture was its mainstay, with over two-thirds of a large population, approximately 8.5 million in 1845, dependent upon it. Of these there was an underclass of more than 2 million 'cottiers', regarded even by contemporaries as below a base poverty line, who received from a farmer a little land on which they might erect a one-roomed, windowless 'cabin' of mud, turf or stone, which they paid for by their labour. Potatoes, which were effectively their only food, were cultivated by the workers in their spare time and with the assistance of their large families. Alternatively the cabin would be built on waste ground and the potato plot rented by the labourer in a system known as 'conacre', by which land was allocated for the time it took a crop to grow. These people, apart from the even more debased landless itinerant 'spailpins' (from the eighteenth-century Gaelic '*spailpín*', or 'penny-a-day worker'), were at the bottom level of a system of sublettings which made the problem of land reform all but intractable.

The land had been acquired during the previous two centuries by mainly English and Scottish investors, who were encouraged to settle as a means of keeping the unruly natives in a quiescent condition. Many, though not all, of the landlords were absentees, and after the alleviation of the Penal Laws a growing minority of them were Catholics. Most followed the widespread custom of subletting. A majority took little interest in their properties except to receive their generally profitable rentals. They tried to emulate the lifestyle of their richer equivalents in Britain, with most of their Big Houses, when they inhabited them, being singularly out of place in their settings. There were honourable exceptions, but the majority well-deserved Louis MacNeice's description of them in *The Poetry of W. B. Yeats* (1941): 'In most cases these houses maintained no culture worth speaking of – nothing but an obsolete bravado, an insidious bonhomie and a way with horses.'

The old system of 'middlemen' who held properties on long leases from the landlords

meant that the number of continuing subten-
ancies grew in geometrical progression. By the
early decades of the nineteenth century these
intermediate holders were being gradually replaced by land agents, who formed a social class
just below that of the landlords and who by the
time of the Famine were mainly professionals.
They were, if possible, more execrated in popular
history than their masters; the agents were
regarded as ruthless and dishonest and were
better known to their clients than the often
remote proprietors. Though there were exceptions, agents were on the whole honest and
often acted as a buffer between the unreasonable
demands of the owners and the misery of the
tenants-at-will. Landlords and middlemen were
usually interested solely in income and there was
little reinvestment of rental income in the
properties. The precariousness of tenure and the
reluctance of tenants to effect any improvements
for fear of rack-renting meant that, although
farms were generally productive, this was despite
generally irresponsible or iniquitous owners.

Visitors to Ireland were appalled by the poverty
they saw among the cottiers, comparing it un-

favourably with the condition of the poor in Asia and Africa. The cabins were likely to be virtually unfurnished, with bales of straw used for bedding, rags for clothes and a system of sharing slightly better raiment for alternate attendance at Sunday worship. Those who lived west of a line from Derry to Waterford were likely to be Gaelic-speaking and unable to read or write it. The *bothóga* might have no window and certainly no chimney; the leaky roof served. Pigs and other livestock, if any were owned, shared the heat from the substantial turf fire and, although the in-habitants were usually dirty and the children slept with little concern for differences of age and sex, there was among these aborigines an inappropriate air of gaiety. They smoked and drank, made music and danced, attended patterns of local saints and fairs and, when removed from their insuperably degrading conditions by voluntary emigration, became noted for their capacity for hard work and harder drink. And, although they were shocked by the dirt and untidiness they saw, the fastidious tourists had to admit that these wretched creatures were on the whole healthy – endemic smallpox, typhus and natal fever being taken into account.

There were cases of equal rural squalor in Britain, as any reading of Dickens, Trollope or Mrs Gaskell will make clear, but these were the mark of uncaring landlords or true fecklessness. Most Irish cottiers were far from feckless, or they would not have survived. Trevelyan's heavily ironic description of the cottier's life – 'a fortnight's planting, a week or ten days' digging and fourteen days' turf-cutting suffice for his subsistence. During the rest of the year he is at leisure to follow his own inclinations' – was grotesquely unfair. The 'subsistence' work was far from easy, especially if the cottier's patch was on bad or rocky land. The cutting, drying, footing and stacking of the huge mounds of turf needed for the long cold seasons took considerably more than a fortnight and the ridge system of potato cultivation was complicated and ecologically sound. Manure was placed under two folds of upturned sods, and when the seed potatoes were placed at regular intervals in the centre of these folds, soil from shallow trenches was piled on top to makes ridges two feet high. It was an effective system but extremely laborious to maintain.

The 'leisure to follow inclinations' meant working for the farmer from whom the cottier had rented the strip, at the next higher stage of subdivision. In the wilder shores of the west and the infertile mountains the work to win a crop was all the harder. Inevitably there was little work to be done during the winter but neither was there opportunity for alternative employment. Scandalous, too, to the righteous English middle classes in the throes of the Second Reformation and settling down to Victorianism under Prince Albert were the improvident early marriages and the overproduction of children among the Irish. The old problem that always afflicted the English was their erroneous belief that they understood the Irish – that they were a kind of less-perfect race of Britons, who with proper guidance might someday be brought to adult, British maturity. As the ballad of later years was to say, 'Won't Mother England be surprised!'

William Allingham's long poem 'Laurence Bloomfield in Ireland' (1864) gives a remarkably frank account of the period, describing Isaac Brown, the absentee landlord of Ballytullagh, as:

> *a man elect...*
> *Who bought and still buys land, none quite*
> *sees how,*
> *Whilst all his shrewdness and success allow.*
> *On Crashton's mortgage he has money lent,*
> *He takes a quiet bill at ten per cent.*

The hamlet itself is 'a windy dwelling-place, rough, lonesome, poor' where:

> *Each cottage rude within-doors as without:*
> *All rude and poor: some wretched – black and bare*
> *And doleful as the cavern of Despair.*

The response of the English authorities to the 'visitation' was inevitably coloured by these, to us, heartless attitudes, and as the problems continued year after year the authorities became more certain that the blight had provided a literally heaven-sent opportunity to purge Ireland of its agricultural evils and establish a proper system based on fiscal – and moral – rectitude.

# 2

## *PHYTOPHTHERA INFESTANS*

The blight that attacked the main source of subsistence of more than 2 million people first appeared in the late summer of 1845. *Phytophthera infestans* was a fungus which was carried by wind to the plant leaves and by rain to the tubers. The unusually wet July had not seemed to affect an excellent crop but by October between a third and half of the yield had been turned into a blackened, noisome pulp. The likely source of the blight was ironically the eastern seaboard of the United States, and countries in Europe from Sweden to Switzerland and as far east as Poland were affected by it. That autumn Ireland was not the worst afflicted, although the 'lumper', which was late maturing, was particularly vulnerable to the blight. (The change from superior 'garden' varieties like the 'black' and the 'apple' to the watery lumper, previously regarded as suitable only for animal fodder, had resulted from the lumper's later maturity, greater yield and tolerance of poorer land.) Yet none of the other countries was so absolutely dependent upon the potato for survival as Ireland.

Potatoes, which were probably not brought to Ireland by Sir Walter Raleigh, were garden crops in the seventeenth century in Leinster and Munster and were known as an excellent means of clearing weeds from ground to be cultivated. The talented tuber played its part in the new science of crop rotation, and during the transition from grazing to tillage that characterised the agricultural economy during the long wars with France at the beginning of the 19th century it became a field crop. Tillage is much more labour-intensive than the relatively leisurely animal husbandry, since nature had provided green Ireland with a mild, damp climate and sufficient grass for grazing. Early marriages and high birth rates provided the necessary surge in population. It was soon realised that the potato was highly nutritious and with milk or fish formed a complete diet for a healthy person – Irish recruits into the army and navy were noticeably taller and healthier than their British equivalents – and adults for whom the potato was a staple ate up to a stone of the vegetable a day.

Since one tiny potato holding could provide subsistence for a large family for the nine months from September to May and the building of primitive shelters was within the power of most labouring men with help from their neighbours, who lived so close, early marriages were the rule and couples' unusual fecundity was credited by some naive observers to the potato as well. (According to the 1841 census, three-quarters of all Irish houses were mud cabins, and of these, 40 per cent consisted of one room.) Part of the crop fed the pigs – those 'gintlemen that paid the rint', in the probably non-native jocose remark of pre-Famine Ireland – and life was possible. The people may have been incredibly poor and lacking in any experience of money, but thanks to the unattractive 'lumper' they had a settled low content.

The war-generated prosperity ceased with the Congress of Vienna in 1815, after which cereals were no longer as profitable a crop as they had been. A move back to livestock rearing was clearly indicated since already, thanks to improved transport facilities, there was much demand for Irish cattle, sheep and pigs on the hoof. Yet the majority of those who could have effected the change – the landlords, middlemen and farmers – preferred to continue with the tillage system since it required no extra effort on their part. For one thing, the reversion to grazing would have required vast clearances such as had been made continuously in the highlands and islands of Scotland since 1800. The same pattern of heavy emigration caused by the clearances was aggravated after Scotland's own potato famine and the inexplicable failure of herring fishing from 1820. In fact the destruction of the Irish masses' only food finally engineered in the grisliest possible way the clearances that agronomy demanded.

It is almost impossible for the layman to avoid making the assumption that there was a causal connection between social conditions in Ireland and the nature of the catastrophe. The population almost doubled between 1791 and

1841, reaching a census figure in the latter year of 8,175,124. It did not seem possible that the ill-managed land could continue to feed and house such a relentlessly increasing population. Yet research has shown that, although the population was still increasing, it had passed its highest rate of gain in 1791; that the mean age of marriage was in fact decreasing; and that in 1844 Ireland was producing enough food for 9 million people. The devastation was caused by the loss of the food that one-third of the people had as sole sustenance and upon which another third partially depended. This first one-third had no intermediary system between themselves and their food; they created their own supply and had no means of obtaining substitutes. The system could have continued except for the *recurring* loss of crop from 1845 to 1852. This *was* a visitation, an awful accident, and as the events of the Famine years showed, no provision had been made for such an eventuality.

Ireland had known famines before: the years 1740–1 were a kind of grisly rehearsal for the drama that was to come a century later, with potato failure, the associated diseases and an even greater proportional mortality rate than in the Great Famine. There had been many at-least-partial crop failures in the first forty years of the nineteenth century, notably in 1816, 1822 and 1831, when the situation had necessitated government intervention. During the first of these outbreaks the Chief Secretary had been the young Robert Peel (1788–1850); he had successfully organised relief measures, finding £250,000 for the purpose. Now, though, bruised by O'Connell's repeal campaigns, he knew Irish conditions sufficiently well to allocate £100,000 for the private purchase of Indian corn and the setting up of a distribution system. The food was not going to be given free; the government could not be seen as a source of dole. The maize would be available at just above cost for those who had the money to buy it, and the knowledge that the government had stores which, if released, would drive down the cost on the open market kept the price of the commercial commodity reasonably low.

The majority of people at risk did not have money to buy food even at its cheapest. Their truck with actual coinage was limited to the cash they had to pay to the landlord's agent on the quarterly gale days. They were allowed to earn enough from public works to save them and their families from starvation. This work was originally intended to improve the island's economy and a programme of building piers and harbours on the rocky south and west coasts and of creating much-needed drainage in the wetlands was proposed. These options were rarely taken up by the local committees who administered the scheme. There were clashes with vested interests and fears that drainage schemes might favour some landlords, to the disadvantage of others. The system lent itself to abuse, with the 'half-grant' advances to the board of works being taken up in many cases where there was no real need, the landlords naturally preferring to spend public money than to use their own.

Most of the labour was done on making new roads and improving existing ones; to some of the labourers working in the open with no warm clothing in the winter and spring of 1845–6 and missing the satisfactory sense of repletion provided by their accustomed diet, the work, which required the digging up of perfectly good boreens, seemed pointless. The local boards were sufficiently imbued with current economic ideas to hesitate doing work of real utility since that would interfere with the 'natural' order and deprive professionals of proper contract work. A relic of those days is a very un-Roman winding road which makes its way round the rocks and lakes of the Rosses of northwest Donegal; it is still called '*bóthar na mine buí*' ('yellow-meal road'). There are many similar roads throughout the country. The high walls built around the outer perimeters of Big Houses and the sections of highway without beginnings or ends are memorials to the disaster nearly as potent as the fields, with their patterns of unmarked stones, that served as Famine cemeteries.

The sulphur-yellow, pebble-hard grain soon known as 'Peel's Brimstone' was unpopular. It required heavy milling and made an unappetising and often indigestible porridge. Those who, in need, tried to ingest it raw suffered dreadfully from bowel complaints and many children and elderly people succumbed. In time sheer need made the stuff acceptable, especially when the millers, on government instruction, added oatmeal to it in a ratio of one to three. Opposition diminished when the authorities published a pamphlet costing a halfpenny with simple cooking instructions for maize. (Even here the government could not countenance any handouts.) The aversion to the porridge turned to acceptance: people ironically preferred the government stuff, which was believed to be superior to maize.

Peel was not as doctrinaire in his economic beliefs as the Whigs who replaced him in the summer of 1846. He did not allow Trevelyan a free rein and was able to impose his system of relief upon the Treasury, if not without opposition. He made no move, however, to prevent the export of Irish grain, even though there was a kind of precedent for such action. Pragmatic as he was, it would not have occurred to him to interfere with 'free' trade, nor to become a purchaser of the Irish crop. His main interest in economics was in the matter of protectionism, notably in what were called the Corn Laws. These measures, which had been introduced in 1815 to favour British producers, prevented the import of foreign grain until a sufficiently high market price had been reached for home produce.

As a manufacturer's son and a true product of the Industrial Revolution, Peel knew that the growing population in Britain needed cheaper bread, and he used the Famine in Ireland as the reason for the repeal of the protective legislation. He succeeded in passing the controversial legislation with the help of some Whigs but it cost him his administration: Lord John Russell (1792–1878) was able to form a minority government with the support of right-wing Tories. The effect of free trade in grain upon the situation in Ireland was necessarily limited since the destitute had no purchasing power, and by the time the country as a whole began to benefit from the new policy, in the spring of 1847, it was much too late for those who had perished from starvation or famine disease.

The summer of 1846 was reached with no serious excess death rate, though the misery of half the population had deepened. Scurvy, which had been unknown thanks to the abundance of Vitamin C in the potato, was now prevalent and children were already showing signs of vitamin deficiency. (The lack of Vitamin A, also present in the bountiful potato, was to cause widespread xerophthalmia in children as the crisis progressed. This disease causes damage to the cornea and can lead to blindness if not treated.) The authorities were quietly congratulating themselves on their handling of the crisis, though there was justifiable criticism of the administration in Dublin. O'Connell's Mansion House committee, founded at Hallowe'en in 1845, when the full venom of the blight had been understood, did not receive the support from the Castle to which it was entitled.

Already Lord Russell's administration, which was much more doctrinaire about laiss*ez-faire* than the Tories, had begun to criticise Peel's relief measures. Trevelyan had found a staunch ally in Sir Charles Wood, later Viscount Halifax (1800–80), the new Chancellor of the Exchequer, and it was clear that with such men in charge of the purse strings relief was to be kept to a minimum. Still, the potato had never failed in two consecutive years before and, although stocks were low and there was still wide distress, there was hope that a renewed crop would blunt the worst miseries of the Famine.

# 3

## BLACK '47

Fr Theobald Mathew (1790–1856), who had persuaded half the adult population of Ireland to abstain from alcohol and who vainly tried to prevent the brewers and distillers from using up grain supplies at the height of the Famine, wrote a much-quoted letter to Trevelyan on 7 August 1846:

> On the 27th of last month, I passed from Cork to Dublin, and this doomed plant bloomed in all the luxuriance of an abundant harvest. Returning on the 3rd instant I beheld with sorrow one wide waste of putrefying vegetation. In many places the wretched people were seated on the fences of their decaying gardens, wringing their hands and wailing the

destruction that had left them foodless.

The blight had returned and this time the failure was virtually total. The population, dependent upon the potato, had always faced hungry summers between the time when the supply of 'old' potatoes had run out and the time when the late lumpers would be ready for digging. Now many were facing an extension of that hunger. Harvests were bad all over Europe and the food supply in Ireland was seriously depleted. The price of grain rose rapidly and the merchants buying up the farmer's excess found that prices in Britain were much better than at home. The export of much-needed grain and the usual quotas of bacon and butter that summer and autumn not unexpectedly caused great anger and would be one of the charges laid against 'England' in future nationalist rhetoric. The shipments by now had to be guarded by military personnel, since terrified and hungry people objected to their means of survival being sent out of the country.

The authorities could not, without special powers – which were unlikely to be granted by the government of the day – have prevented these exports. The idea was almost unthinkable and, besides, the food was needed in England! The amount exported – the food equivalent of about 9 per cent of the lost potato crop – would not have prevented the famine that followed, but it would have saved some lives in the period between August and the arrival of new supplies of maize in the winter of 1846–7. A remarkable inconsistency in Irish matters continued to afflict the establishment in London. By the terms of the Act of Union Ireland was a constituent part of the United Kingdom, yet food shipped from there was regarded not as ordinary market produce coming from one part of the country to the other but rather as foreign imports. The Treasury objected to allocating 'English' money to help the afflicted 'potatophagi', as the London *Times* referred to the lesser Hibernian breeds, which, the paper argued, were kept back from full maturity by 'the blindness of Irish patriotism, the short-sighted indifference of petty landlords or the random recklessness of government ben- evolence'. The benevolence ceased: the Russell administration decided that all relief schemes were to be financed by local rates and managed by local committees, with all the attendant likelihood of inefficiency, local difficulties and corruption.

The numbers of people on relief works rose from 114,000 in October to 570,000 in January 1847 and reached a total of 750,000 by March. The winter was particularly cold and wild, and cottiers, who were used to relatively cosy firesides and full bellies, found themselves doing appallingly laborious and meaningless work, in near-rags and often without food from morning to night. The righteous Trevelyan devised a means of saving the exchequer money by imposing a system of piecework rather than a flat rate. This meant in practice that all but the strongest could not earn enough to feed themselves, let alone their large families. The soaring price of maize further aggravated the calamity. The news from Ireland grew blacker every week – reluctant as Trevelyan and Wood were to believe it. Thousands were dying, and with 750,000 labourers engaged on piecework in pointless public works there was no labour to do the normal farm work and turf-saving. It was suggested that the public workers should have leave to engage in seeding and turf-cutting, and be paid for the work, but the Treasury could not countenance the idea of paying people to work on their own land. (It was then that Trevelyan made his knowledgeable observation about the work-span of the wily, lazy Irish cottier.)

The coastal dwellers who might have hoped for food from the sea found that continuous gale-force southwesters made it impossible to risk going out in curraghs. Many had pawned or sold their nets and lines and were driven to eating shellfish. In sand-dune shore, a winter gale can still expose a high hill of shells, a mark of the communal eating of the time. Only extreme hunger would have conquered the littoral distaste for *iasc sliogach*: throughout the country herring had never been eaten except as sauce for the potato. Edible seaweeds, such as carrageen moss, sloak and dulse – the first two boiled to make a kind of cornflour, the last dried and eaten raw and still prized as a recreational food in parts of Ulster – saved some lives. In these years the rocks were stripped clean and the recovered distaste for shellfish was never fully overcome among the people.

It was clear by the arctic spring of 1847 that the system of public works was not working; too many people were literally falling dead and if inquests were held the government – often nominally Russell – was held responsible for the fatalities. The schemes had ceased by March but the promised direct-feeding organisation did not begin until the end of May. There was nothing to bridge the hiatus except the efforts of private charities or what could be made available under the existing poor-law regulations. The efficacy of all relief schemes depended upon the efficiency of local organisers. Where the parish priest or curate was active and the local government officials responsible, a sufficient amount of nourishing food kept the needy populace alive. The problem was that in large tracts of Connacht, the region hardest hit, there was little or no infrastructure by which the public-works system could be made to work justly. Later, when the soup kitchens were set up, the means of distributing adequate food to those most in need was inefficient. There was a shortage of clergy and other community leaders in the west, and the landlords were, with notable exceptions, irresponsible and often absentee. Many of their agents took no responsibility for the cottiers, and even the tenant farmers, most of whom were Catholic, seemed to find no reason to help the starving sharecroppers on their lands. In fact the tenant farmers were most severe in pursuing those caught trying to steal turnips from their fields; they shot intruders, assuming, often correctly, that they would not be regarded as doing more than defending their property.

The lead in food distribution had been taken by the Religious Society of Friends in November 1846. In true Quaker tradition the Friends acted out of pure humanity and gave soup and maize porridge to all who sought it. The British Association also organised relief; among the charitable donations received by them was one of £2,000 (the equivalent of £80,000 in today's money) by Queen Victoria. (One of the strongly held myths among fervid nationalists, especially abroad, was that her sole contribution to relief funds was £5, the same as she gave to a dogs' home.) Worthy as these efforts were – and it must be said that a number of landlords, including the Marquesses of Waterford and Sligo and the Colthursts of Blarney, to their credit set up their own relief schemes – the situation required national effort on the part of the government. The spurs to alternative options had been the success, limited only by their resources, of the voluntary charities (and the fact that the public-works system was not only inefficient but also costly).

The necessary 'soup kitchen' legislation had been passed as early as February 1847, but the preparing of perceived bureaucratic needs in the form of account books and meal tickets meant that there was an appalling delay in its implementation. (The actual hardware had been in place since the spring.) The first dole did not take place until May, in a mercifully dry and warm summer, and the initiative soon proved effective within the limitations of local conditions, the far west and south-west again being disadvantaged because of the lack of local organisers of sufficient integrity and efficiency. It was soon realised that the distribution of uncooked food did not achieve its humanitarian purpose. Many of those in need had no means of cooking it and, as we have noted, the hard grains of maize eaten raw had a dire effect upon badly upset digestive systems. It was found, too, that many of those who received the uncooked food sold it for tea, liquor or tobacco. By August 3 million people were having cooked meals supplied and – in contrast to the public-works system – adequate nourishment was at last being obtained. It is hard for our disaster-conscious society to understand what a great mental shift the idea of 'free' food supplied by the central authority represented. To apply Dr Johnson's remark in an entirely different context: 'It is not done well; but you are surprised to find it done at all.'

In the private sector the Friends and the British Association had used local Church of Ireland clergy to act as honest distributors of relief, and the majority carried out their philanthropic work – where possible with the cooperation of local priests – with exemplary

Christianity and often at the risk of their lives, since the middle classes were particularly susceptible to the now-epidemic typhus. Compared with the ministers, priests had huge congregations, and their care of souls left them little time to engage in the organisation of relief. Most were happy to trust their separated brethren to deal with the corporal needs of their distressed flocks. The agencies had no proselytising aim, being concerned only with relieving the affliction of fellow creatures of God. However, a small number of extreme evangelistic ministers, fervently believing in their providentialist way that the Hunger was a visitation sent from an ultimately benevolent God, saw no harm in cooperating with that Famine God in offering the means of survival to the misguided. The apocalypse was seen as an opportunity for the erring to repent their wrong-headedness and for their famished children to have their straying feet set on the path of righteousness, strengthened by righteous soup.

Like so many aspects of the Famine, the extent of 'souperism' was later greatly exaggerated, the sense of advantage being taken of the stricken inflating the perceived evil. The most serious result of the charges of souperism was that in some cases agencies that would have abhorred proselytism were taken as being evangelistic. Catholic priests, not without their own sense of providentialism, were often not precise enough in their denunciation of proselytising bodies, and many genuine Protestant philanthropists were wrongly accused of the practice. Not only did poor people, scared of disobeying their priests, die unnecessarily of hunger but also an anti-Anglican acrimony persisted for decades after the end of the Famine. Though 'lower' and more scripturally orientated than their brethren in England, Irish Anglicans were generally tolerant of Catholicism; they were latitudinarian rather than hotly evangelistic and deplored the animosity of a post-Famine, somewhat triumphalist Roman Church.

The uncharacteristic clemency of the weather in the summer of 1847 meant that the blight did not recur that autumn. The authorities, still unaware of the nature of the infection, assumed that the crisis had passed. There had, however, been little planting done in the Famine areas: the total acreage planted was only a tenth of the norm, and there were practically no healthy seeds and no healthy labourers to make the 'lazy-beds'. Immediately the government soup kitchens were closed and, 'charity fatigue' having set in in Britain and America, independent relief was scaled down. The blight struck again savagely in 1848 and to a lesser extent in 1849 but by then starvation was not the only killer. The endemic typhus became epidemic and the crush of population in the congested districts of the west and south meant that the disease, which was carried by infected lice, spread like plague. The daily queues for food and the complete lack of sanitary facilities – few ever managed a change of clothing and personal hygiene deteriorated – meant that here, as well, conditions were ideal for the spread of disease.

In fact typhus was not as deadly among the poor, since they had built up some kind of immunity over the years; it proved lethal, however, to the clergy and civil servants who in their different ways ministered to the 3 million affected by the Famine. The hundreds of thousands of the poor who died succumbed mainly to relapsing fever, a disease caused by infection by the bacillus of syphilis and yaws. The high fever and the mortality rate caused the two separate scourges to be taken as the same 'famine disease', and since both were spread by lice and both were deadly, the population were in no position to distinguish between them. When in the next chapters of the tragedy the poor were crowded into workhouses or, hoping for salvation by emigration, onto even more crowded ships, the bacilli found ideal conditions for wreaking their havoc. Other illnesses associated with the calamity were anasarca – a form of diffused dropsy – and famine dysentery. In the excess death rate of a million or more resulting from the disaster, it is assumed that at least two-thirds died from disease.

# 4

## . . . ANOTHER FOR THE POOR

When the late summer of 1847 proved blight-free, Russell's riven cabinet and the Treasury assumed that the crisis was over and set about dealing with the millions who, wasted by hunger and disease, were still their unwished-for responsibility. They were determined that no more British money would be spent on the feckless Irish and that relief would be funded by the Irish landlords and tenants through the rate-financed poor law. The poor-law system had been set up in 1838 as one of the minor concessions won for Ireland by O'Connell in return for his support of the Whigs under Melbourne and Russell after the informal Lichfield House 'pact'. The report of the commission of Archbishop Whately (1787–1863) – which found that at least 2.5 million people needed assistance for some weeks of each year and recommended major schemes of land improvement and assisted voluntary emigration – was rejected as wildly expensive.

The new commissioners were told to limit their efforts to the relief of destitution and not poverty but were given powers to set up a system not unlike that established in England in 1834, with some notable differences. There was no given right to relief, as had existed in England since the seventeenth century, and the workhouses would not be responsible for any outdoor relief. The country was divided into 130 'unions' of parishes, with a workhouse in each. The workhouses were well-built if interiorly unattractive complexes and, though clean, were made as uncomfortable as possible, so as to be places of last resort. They were constructed to a standard design, with infirmaries at the rear of the main dormitories, and lasted so well that some still form the nuclei of modern hospitals. The sexes, even children, were segregated, members of the same family never seeing each other except across the aisles at Sunday services. Breaches of discipline were punished by flogging or periods of isolation; the inmates wore a special uniform and the food provided was deliberately monotonous. The men worked eight to ten hours a day breaking stone, the women sewed and the children were given a limited and strongly pietistic education. The Irish did not take to regimentation and in normal times able-bodied people, no matter how poor, would not cross the thresholds of these cold, charitable prisons. The usual workhouse population consisted of the old, the young and the ill.

The commissioners always insisted that provision was adequate for non-critical situations – there was accommodation for about 100,000 inmates – but the law did not provide even for limited emergencies, let alone a catastrophe of the kind they had so soon to deal with. In the spring of 1847 three-quarters of the institutions were full. Lacking a law of settlement, the Irish had no right to relief, and when the workhouses were full obligation on the part of the poor-law commissioners ceased. In practice, at the height of the Famine many guardians ignored the law and, either because of compassion or fear – since men dying of hunger grew desperate – extra accommodation was somehow found and out-door relief was administered in spite of the rules.

The successful running of the scheme de-pended upon local money obtained from the rates. The government must have known that this was one piece of theory that did not work in practice. The larger unions, with the greater populations, were those in the poorest parts of the country and were therefore the ones most affected by the disruption. Donegal, Monaghan, Cavan, Fermanagh, parts of the midlands, most of Connacht and a large part of Munster had huge destitute populations, the greatest likeli-hood of ownership by absentee landlords and consequent difficulty in the collection of rates. The adequacy of relief was dependent upon local conditions. If the landlord took his respon-sibilities seriously and had the money to do something about the state of his tenants, then hunger – and sometimes even disease – was averted. One such was the Catholic landlord George Henry Moore (d. 1870), the father of the Irish novelist and playwright George Augus-tus Moore (1852–1933). George Henry owned

Moore Hall near Lough Carra in County Mayo and in spite of receiving virtually no rent during the whole Famine period carried out no evictions. He was a well-known racehorse owner and trainer, and the reason given at the time for his forbearance was that he had won so much money on the Calcutta Derby that he could afford to wait for better times.

A notable contrast was his neighbour George Charles Bingham, Lord Lucan (1800–88), progenitor of the late-twentieth-century's most famous absentee landlord and subsequently a famous evictor. He had actively encouraged the building of the Castlebar Union on his land, expecting that it would soon go bankrupt and he would thus secure possession of some fine buildings. He was chairman of the board of guardians, with a conveniently quiescent committee, and had the workhouse shut, saying that there was no money left, when in October 1846 throngs of desperate people tried to gain admission. He would allow no form of relief to be given and was accused of allowing the inmates of the union to starve to death. Later he was found to have been one of the chief causes of the lack of cash since he had paid no rates.

Another turn of the screw was the passing in June 1847 of the Irish Poor Law Extension Act. Its intention was to penalise landlords for their absenteeism and the irresponsible sub-division of their estates, and, with its unprofitable proliferation of tiny holdings and the setting up of Irish agriculture on a sound capitalist base, it was a deliberate step towards the goal of ending subsistence farming. The doublethink which characterised English thinking was never so obvious as here: the collecting of these local taxes had always been a difficult business but now, with the rate in some cases tripling, it became dangerous. The collectors went in fear of their lives and, although they had sufficient authority to wrest money from the farmers and middlemen, the landlords when encountered could usually face them down. Inevitably it was the poor who suffered. The rate money was required not for the normal running of a lumbering if working system but to save the lives of hundreds of thousands of people. Even while the measure was being put into practice word had come from Schull in west Cork that

7,332 people had died in six contiguous parishes between September 1846 and September 1847. This, allowing for normal mortality, was one-sixth of the population. The same pattern was repeated all over the 'Famine' areas, and the figure of 1.3 million deaths in that period that these proportions would signify if applied nationally might not be too inaccurate. True, most of Ulster and Leinster were not afflicted in so severe a fashion, but there were many places where excess mortality was even worse than in Schull.

Under the grand plan that Russell's cabinet (which contained such intractable Irish landlords as Lord Palmerston, his Foreign Secretary, and Lord Clanricarde, Postmaster-General) devised, a majority in the House and in Trevelyan's Treasury had visualised that some of the 'lazy' cottiers would become agricultural labourers on farms of sufficient acreage to warrant proper investment and generate rich profits. It was intended that these labourers should have adequate housing and sufficient wages to pay their rents and care for their families. The rationalists did not much care what would happen to the great surplus of workers that would result from the clearances, nor did they understand the almost obsessional significance that the holding of land had for the Irish peasants. By this logical means the sordid and recurring problems of Irish agriculture would be solved and the ugliness, both moral and visual, of strip farming and rural cabins would be literally extirpated from the fair hills of Erin.

One clause of the bill, known as the 'quarter-acre' – though more commonly by the name of its proposer, Sir William Gregory (1816–92), the Tory MP for Dublin City – was to prove cruelly effective in achieving the clearances that were seen as necessary for the desired agricultural reforms. Gregory is now mainly famous as the gambling landlord of Coole Park and husband of the young Augusta Persse (1852–1932), who taught Yeats how to write plays and helped him found the Abbey Theatre. Gregory's amendment, which he successfully forced, with the support of most Irish MPs, on the Whig administration, prohibited the relief from the poor rates of anyone occupying more than a quarter-acre of land and of their dependants. (This latter refinement was rescinded in May

1848 when the authorities' detachment crumbled before the charge of imposing deliberate starvation upon the innocent.) The effect was to impose the extra evil of eviction upon many thousands of smallholders.

Meanwhile, more people died of famine and its associated diseases; many who were entitled to succour literally did not have the strength to make their way to the workhouses. Their bodies often lay unburied – a spartan meal for the wild dogs who had turned scavengers – their lips green from eating grass and other weeds. The failure of the 1848 potato crop meant that almost a million people were in receipt of workhouse relief and the rate of workhouse death stayed at the level of 2,500 a week. Ireland was in the grip of a terrible despair. As Mitchel put it, 'A calm still horror was over all the land. Go where you would, in the heart of the town or in the church, on the mountainside or on the level plain, there was the stillness and heavy pall-like feeling of the chamber of death.' But there was more misery to come.

# 5

## GREGORYISM

The Poor Law Extension Act of 1847 permitted outdoor relief, against the tenor of previous legislation, but because it required that all relief be financed by local rates it actually limited the amount of relief that was available. More seriously – though comparisons of seriousness at that extreme are academic – it spurred many landlords to clear people off, in Trevelyan's words written in *The Irish Crisis,* 'the small patches of lands which supported a family when laid down to potatoes.' He continued:

[they] are insufficient for the purpose when laid down to corn or any other kind of produce; and corn cultivation requires capital and skill which the cottier and conacre tenants do not possess. The

position occupied is no longer tenable,
and it is necessary for them either to
become substantial farmers or to live by
the wages of their labour.

The unemotional reification of the Irish poor by
the British establishment of the period could
hardly be better summarised than in that last
sentence, though the often-quoted statement of
Lord Clarendon (1800–70), who was famous as
an impartial Viceroy (1847–52), in a letter
written to Russell in August 1847, runs it close:
'We shall equally be blamed for keeping [the
Irish] alive or letting them die and we have only
to select between the censures of the Economists
or the Philanthropists . . . '

The chance of 2 million surplus labourers
finding work was only slightly less unlikely than
their hope of becoming 'substantial farmers'.
The method by which the desired clearances
would be effected was known at the time as
'Gregoryism', though the infamous 'quarter-
acre' clause was only part of the means of
achieving this end. This clause provided that no
tenant holding more than that tiny acreage was

eligible for relief and spelt the end for tens of thousands of small farmers. The law did not seem to see that the holders of, say, a third of an acre or even half an acre were in straits as dire as the 'lucky' ones protected by the law. The refusal of relief applied also to these people's families, as an ever-more-potent lever than that directed against the head of the family. The distressed tried to get round this inhumane legislation by claiming to be widows or orphans – a likely enough condition at the time – while the father hid out in his hovel. Many members of the workhouse board connived at the deception but there were others whose stiff-necked right-eousness would not countenance such 'cheating'. The outcry against its inhumanity finally ended the application of the clause to women and children by the following May but by then thousands had been pressurised into yielding to their malign fate. As soon as the stricken families had left their holdings, the cabins were levelled and the lazy-beds ploughed over.

The other clause of the act that en-couraged eviction was that which made landlords responsible for all the rates on properties with

The home of a typical rural Irish family before the Famine
(Guildhall Library)

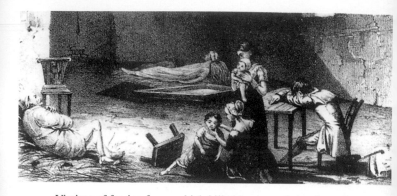

Victims of famine fever, which killed huge numbers of people in 'Black '47'. There was no cure for the disease; only adequate nutrition could limit its spread

A famine funeral in Skibbereen, County Cork, in January 1847 – one of the many such funerals that took place that year
(National Library of Ireland)

A farming family seeking to avoid eviction in 1847

This soup kitchen in Cork, run by a branch of the Dublin-based Quaker Central Relief Committee, distributed around 6,800 litres of soup a day to the poor in January 1847

The village of Tullig, near Kilrush, County Clare, as drawn by an artist from the *Illustrated London News* in late 1849. The magazine reported that 'the sketch is not of a deserted village . . . for wretched beings who once viewed it as an abode of plenty and peace still linger and hover about it – but of a destroyed village.'

(Illustrated London News Picture Library)

an annual rental of £4 or less. Inevitably this affected some proprietors more than others. Three-quarters of all holdings in County Mayo, for example, were subject to the £4 clause, and since Mayo might well be considered the blackest of all the Famine areas, the rates bill to be carried by landlords was heaviest. Removals – to use for the moment a decently unspecific word – of tenants from smallholdings was greatest in Clare, Mayo, Galway and Kerry; they were made in numbers which accounted for a third of all permanent clearances in the Famine period. Police records – they and the army (for which money was always found by the Treasury) were always present at evictions where resistance was expected – were not kept until 1849 but they show that during the next six years 250,000 people were made homeless. Most historians accept that an equal number were dislodged in the years 1846–8.

Where possible, landlords preferred their clients to leave voluntarily. In some cases full fares on board ships bound for Canada and Australia were given as a kind of compensation. Francis Spaight, a parvenu proprietor, removed

1,400 people from his land in this way. William Steuart Trench (1808–72), who was land agent for three of the country's biggest proprietors – the Marquis of Bath, Lord Landsdowne and Lord Digby – and wrote one of the best books about the period, *Realities of Irish Life* (1868), successfully shipped nearly 5,000 people from Landsdowne's estates in Kenmare. After much Dickensian mismanagement by the Court of Chancery, Major Denis Mahon inherited an estate in Strokestown, County Roscommon, which was heavily in debt (by about £2 million in today's money) and full of struggling cottiers. Rents had not been collected for years and were now unrecoverable. He took advice from his cousin, John Ross Mahon, a successful businessman, who agreed to act as his agent and arranged for 900 of his tenants to go voluntarily to Canada. Ross Mahon travelled with them to Liverpool and made sure that they had sufficient provisions for the voyage. In fact many of them died en route, and in an unconnected incident Major Mahon was murdered. One philanthropic landlord, Vere Foster, who had property in County Louth, set up a fund to help emigrants, contributing £10,000 of his own money to it. Later, after hearing of the conditions on board the emigrant ships, he travelled to America three times to find out for himself what they were like. His reports to parliamentary committees were instrumental in laying down minimum standards for the ships.

Not everybody was amenable to assisted passages and most landlords were not especially worried what happened to their tenants once they had been evicted and their habitations demolished. Since many of the evictions occurred during the winter, some of the dispossessed died of exposure. One notorious case was that of the Kilrush Union in west Clare, where the landlord Colonel Vandeleur issued 6,000 notices to quit in November 1847 and the work was carried out by his ruthlessly efficient agent Marcus Keane. It took little time for Keane's eviction gang to level the houses, and little quarter was given. By the end of 1848 the population of the union had been reduced by 27 per cent to 60,000. The evicted, women and children included, had literally no place to go since other estate tenants were forbidden by law to take them in. The stronger ones took to the roads and formed the nucleus of Ireland's travelling population, others tried to find places in the overcrowded and bankrupt workhouses, while some, with incredible optimism, made their slow way to the embarkation ports, hoping somehow to earn the passage money for themselves and their families.

In Kilrush, the poor-law inspector, Captain Arthur Kennedy, whose six-year-old daughter found iconic fame in an *Illustrated London News* engraving showing her distributing clothes to the poor, was so incensed by his experiences that, as he recalled years later, ' . . . there were days in that western country when I came back from scenes of eviction so maddened by the sights of hunger and misery I had seen in the day's work that I felt disposed to take the gun from behind my door and shoot the first landlord I met'. This from a phlegmatic Ulsterman! The egregious Lord Lucan was also to the fore, crying that 'he would not breed paupers to pay priests' – apparently unaware of the contradiction in his words. He expelled 2,000 people from his holdings in Ballinrobe, County Mayo, alone. This pattern was repeated all over his

30,000 acres, as he depopulated whole townlands and set most of the potato strips for grazing.

Once the example was given, there were few landlords who did not use the prevailing atmosphere of desensitisation of feelings to clear their own unprofitable and expensive small–holdings. They argued that they did this for their own survival, unaware of the irony of their use of the word in the present circumstances. Among the numbers of the evicted were the hated middlemen, who were crushed between the demands of the head landlords and the lack of income from below. Their profits had come from the excess of rents collected over that required by the proprietors. Now there was no income from below and the responsibility that many of them had contractually undertaken for paying rates on the property bankrupted them much more quickly than it did the head land–lords. The class which had been such a feature of Irish rural life for two centuries now disappeared from the scene, lost among the dispossessed and as likely to have emigrated as their late clients.

Death and emigration achieved for the Irish

landholders who survived the biblical seven years of the 'visitation' the desired consolidation of holdings. The number of farms of one to five acres, which had previously occupied 45 per cent of Irish land, declined by up to two-thirds, while that of larger farms multiplied. Livestock farming in medium-sized holdings increased across the country but the west was still characterised by subsistence farming. The fears of bankruptcy that drove many proprietors to extremes of 'extermination', to use the contemporary word for the savage evictions, were not illusory. One-tenth of all large landlords went bankrupt; 874 estates had to be taken over by Chancery and, when the Encumbered Estates Act of 1849 made it possible to sell mortgaged land, many estates were sold to a new breed of farming entrepreneurs. For the mass of the ordinary people, however, the trauma of the Great Hunger was to persist, and in the years 1845–70 3 million of these were to suffer it in exile.

# 6

## '. . . FOR TO SEEK A HOME/
## ON THE SHORES OF AMERIKAY'

Even before the Famine, voluntary emigration from Ireland, especially to the New World, had been established as a significant feature of Irish life. It is reckoned that between 1815 − when with the ending of the Napoleonic Wars the long economic slump set in − and the first appearance of the blight, a million people had left the country to seek better lives. In 1841 there were 400,000 Irish-born people living in Britain, with Irish quarters in Manchester, Glasgow, Birmingham, Cardiff and London. The city that was most conscious of the Irish was Liverpool, which had become the main port of disembarkation for Irish emigrants and provided the best opportunity for a transatlantic berth. In 1847, at the height of the Hunger,

300,000 sailed to Britain because the desperate bush telegraph of the poor had told them that their kind were better treated there, with three meals a day in the workhouses and the chance of meat on Sundays. They soon became aware of the economic slump in Britain and Australia and concentrated their efforts on making it to the United States.

The half million or so Irish who were already established there were socially somewhat above the level of those fleeing from the Famine; the 'lace-curtain' term had not yet been coined but there were a few who had left the ranks of the working class and had assumed middle-class respectability. There was some prejudice against these immigrants because of their religion; the social norm was the white Anglo-Saxon Protestant and the great majority of Irish immigrants in the century before 1815 had been Ulster Presbyterians, who had seen, like so many others, the New World as a land of economic opportunity and a place where they would not suffer the disabilities associated with their nonconformity. Their part in the Revolutionary War and in the establishment of the republican United States was well known but their tolerance of Catholicism, especially low Irish Catholicism, was limited.

The regularity and continuity of Irish emigration to America had established an effective traffic system: ships with empty holds had plenty of space for human ballast on their return to the East Coast ports of Boston and New York, among others. Succeeding waves of emigrants found things easier as the numbers of settlers increased, and although the voyages were frightful, lasting up to ten weeks and featuring appalling conditions, the emigrants were sure of a kind of welcome from their fellows to tide them over the first, upsetting period of their new lives. The ships to the States, especially if American, were regarded as safer and cleaner than those to other destinations. The other land that beckoned emigrants was Canada, with its savage winters and terrifying, seemingly infinite spaces. The ships that plied to Halifax and Quebec were less well-run than those to America, but the fares, at £4, were £2 cheaper than on the ships bound for Boston.

The concept of the 'land of promise' did not affect the Irish only: the drive west was part of a general north European sense of new opportunity – of moving away from the tired old world, with its increasing populations and diminishing natural resources. Ireland's primitive agricultural economy and its overpopulation with respect to the management of its resources made it very susceptible to the siren song of a veritable Hy-Brasil to the west. When the Famine came, with its hunger, disease and destruction of the old economy, flight seemed the only hope of survival. Between 1845 and 1870, 3 million Irish people left Ireland for good, the majority to settle in American cities. The oddity of a largely rural influx settling in city slums is best understood by the fact that farming in America was very different from at home and that, although the emigrants had lived in the country, the nature of the economy meant that the 'Famine' areas were also the most congested. As the Irish proverb put it, *Ar scáth a chéile a mhaireas na daoine* ('People live in each other's shadows'), and it should not be forgotten that life among the strip farmers would have been insupportable without mutual assistance.

By 1847 a large number of the Irish emigrants were already affected by the famine fevers, and outbreaks of typhus were noted in the main cities of Britain. In Liverpool, with jails and workhouses filled to capacity, a public subscription was raised to send as many Irish as possible back home. The conditions on board ship, with lice spreading typhus and dysentery symptoms making a fetid atmosphere worse, are almost unthinkable to modern minds. Again, on the ships bound for Canada conditions were likely to be much worse, with poorer rations and an absence of clean water. The quarantine station Grosse Ile in the St Laurence River was the scene of many deaths during the summer of 1847. The medical superintendent Dr Douglas put the mortality rate at fifty a day at the height of the epidemic, and 5,424 people were buried on the island. In many cases children survived to fill Canadian orphanages.

Inevitably those emigrants who were 'evicted into emigration', with passages paid by such landlords as Mahon, Landsdowne, de Vesci, Gore-Booth and his near-neighbour Palmerston, were sent to Canada because the fare to that country was cheaper than that to America. The emigrants' condition when they arrived in Canada was so pitiable that there was a public outcry. Four hundred and sixty-eight of Palmerston's tenants from east Sligo were sent off in the *Aeolus* to St John, New Brunswick; they were described by the medical superintendent there as 'the most helpless and destitute of any who have landed in this port in the last five years'. Yet the emigrants from Lissadell – Gore-Booth's estate – who came later that year on the same ship thanked 'our ever-to-be-remembered late landlord, Sir Robert Gore-Booth, Bart., Sligo: he was always kind to his tenants; it was not tyranny which forced us to emigrate – it was the loss of crops for two years.' This grand encomium, which was hardly spontaneous, must have pleased Gore-Booth's revolutionary granddaughter Countess Markiewicz. A similar letter was sent by Palmerston's Mullaghmore emigrants, and it was noted that these emigrants were able to send £2,000 home the following year. Perhaps the Canadian authorities exaggerated; they certainly had to cope with an emergency whose demands were well beyond their resources. Palmerston himself was shaken out of his aristocratic phlegm sufficiently by this affair to defend himself in Parliament – his reputation as a landlord had until then been good. He laid the blame for the situation on his agents, who in turn blamed 'the exigencies of the voyage'.

Most emigrants who landed in Canada attempted to make their way on foot across the border, via the strongly Yankee and Protestant states of Maine and New Hampshire, to join one of the Irish communities in the American cities of the northeast – Philadelphia, Baltimore or Chicago, which had many Irish inhabitants since the building by the 'tarriers' of the canals around the Great Lakes. Many of the emigrants died of fatigue and exposure, unable to face the rigours of the winter. Indeed the life expectancy, from the time of their arrival in America, of all but the young and healthy was not much more than five years. The life they faced in the slums of Boston and New York was miserable. Conditions were marginally better than at home; few starved, but mortality, from slum diseases and malnutrition, was high. Many sank into a state of moral degradation that was unknown at home; crime and prostitution were rife and alcohol was cheap. Those who tried to better themselves had to face shame, as well as discrimination and violence from such extreme Protestant groups as the 'Know Nothings'. Incredibly, the emigrants gradually forced their way out of their ghettos, using their discovered political clout. The history of their early struggles has murky elements but with the combined strength of an active Catholic clergy and less respectable 'bosses' they survived. It is against this background that the glory of having the great-grandson of a Famine emigrant become president is most clearly seen.

The emigrants, apart from those who were evicted by landlords, were not the very poorest, however destitute they may have seemed to the transatlantic officials; the fare even to Canada represented several years' wages. Some, hearing of economic recovery in Australia enhanced by the discovery of gold in Bathurst and Ballarat in 1851, liquidated all their meagre assets to find the £14 for the long voyage to New South Wales. There were many ticket-of-leave and time-expired Irish convicts from the penal colonies of Botany Bay, near Sydney, and Van Diemen's Land (later Tasmania) who had settled there. The expectancy of safe arrival and the welcome of fellow country-men made it a popular landfall. Some ingenious emigrants at the height of the Famine had secured passage by committing the right kind of felony –

sufficient to have them transported, but not with too severe a prison sentence.

What startled observers, including many in Britain, who had dismissed the Irish peasant as a kind of subhuman with simian features, as *Punch* generally portrayed him, were the remarkable amounts of money (£1 million in 1850) that came eastwards across the ocean again, either in small amounts of cash to help relatives at home and to repay loans or in the form of prepaid tickets. 'American money' was to continue to flow home for many decades. Conditions steadily improved, and when steamships became sufficiently reliable for the crossing the time at sea was greatly reduced. By the turn of the century emigration was continuing unabated; the poor exiles from Erin were travelling, still in steerage, but in 'grand Allen liners'. The effect of so many Irish-born people living abroad – 3 million in 1890 – was to be politically significant in the seventy years after the end of the Great Hunger. The shores of Amerikay did not seem so far away, and as Edward Senior, a poor-law commissioner, prophetically put it in 1850, 'Everybody has one leg over the Atlantic.'

# 7

## GENOCIDE?

By the 1880s it was discovered that a compound of lime and copper sulphate, when sprayed on the leaves of the potato plants, prevented the blight. Patrick Kavanagh's poem 'Spraying the Potatoes', with the lines, 'Remembering the lime and copper smell/Of the spraying barrel . . .' takes on an extra poignancy, and it was no accident that his requiem for agricultural sterility should have been called *The Great Hunger*. The Famine became a part of the dark folk memory of the Irish – both those who stayed at home in a fundamentally changed country and the millions who over the next hundred years 'spread the grey wing upon every tide'. The census returns for 1851 put the population at 6.5 million, whereas extrapolation from 1841 trends would have given a figure of 9 million.

The steadily increasing Irish population in the

United States, especially after their impressive showing in both armies in the Civil War (1861–5) and their growing commercial and political confidence, began to consider the causes of the Famine and had no difficulty in apportioning blame for it. Their views were conditioned by the fiercely effective, if not entirely just, propaganda of journalists like Mitchel and they had no doubts that they or their parents were victims of a great wrong. Famine ballads became part of the repertoire of the sentimental concerts and at-homes in the 'Irish' cities; most of these ballads demanded vengeance for the tragedy. Perhaps the one that had the greatest impact was 'Old Skibbereen', which purported to recall the plight of the County Cork town where the union built to house 800 had 2,800 inmates in 1848, where it was said the markets were full of food in a town where people dead from hunger often lay for days in the streets unburied and where the death rate was higher than anywhere else in the country. The ballad in fact mentions none of these things and deals with an unspecified eviction in which 'They set my roof on fire with their cursed English spleen' and ends with the cry:

*I'll be the man to lead the van beneath the
 flag so green
When loud and high we'll raise the cry –
 'Remember Skibbereen!'*

The cry was to be heard by a minority in succeeding generations right up to the present day, although the ballad may not be about the Famine period at all. There was no hesitation about believing it, because the greener Americans had it as a fact of faith that the Famine had been created by 'English spleen' to extirpate the Irish. Continuous support for armed struggle at home, from a safe 3,000 miles away in America, was a means of easing atavistic rage and, unlike the individuals who stayed at home with merely local preoccupations, the Irish-Americans developed a concept of Ireland as a whole – a country whose ancient wrongs at the hands of the English for many centuries needed to be avenged.

The reaction of survivors at home was rather more complicated; they did not have the Irish-Americans' simple, visceral conviction that England was to blame. (The concept of 'Britain' was a sophistication too far.) Though few were untouched by the visitation – typhus decimated the better-off as well as the poor – many were in no danger of death and quite a number of the native Irish actually benefited from the clearances. It was not until considerations of survival gave way to a kind of normality by the mid-1850s and there was time to consider the events of the previous decade that blame began to be assigned to landlords, 'sheriffs', policemen, soldiers, middlemen, soupers and workhouse masters – all *local* objects of hatred.

Historians who have studied the huge archive of Famine memories collected by the Folklore Commission in the 1930s have noted that, although terrible stories of the Hunger abound, the contributors tend to minimise the horrors in their own localities while painting much blacker pictures of neighbouring parishes. This may have been a means of retrospectively allaying pain but it is also rooted in a kind of guilt on the part of the contributors that they survived. The success of the Catholic Church in the decades immediately after the Famine owes much to the same kind of feeling. A shocked people needed little prompting to believe that the visitation was in some way due to their immoral behaviour, and sermons from the pulpits of the many fine churches and cathedrals that were begun in the 1840s and continued to be built during the terrible years did not need to be subtle. The effect was to create a docile laity for a clergy that was entering upon its period of greatest power and influence.

In the 1850s the number of priests increased by 20 per cent and the number of nuns rose by 50 per cent. These were rather better behaved than some of their predecessors, and if the church-based services notably lacked the gaiety of pilgrimages, 'patterns' and other events where religion and folklore mingled, they were undoubtedly more devotional. Masses, benedictions, recitations of the Rosary, stations of the cross, novenas and retreats replaced bonfires and holy wells. In religion as with most other aspects of Irish life, the events of 1845–52 did not change things but instead accelerated certain tendencies. The 'devotional' revolution had begun with the Catholic Relief Acts, but a severely traumatised laity gladly accepted the opportunity for repentance and expiation. The care of the Church and the nature of the sermons, with their even-handed balance of the infinite justice and infinite mercy of God, undoubtedly healed some of the trauma. The role of the priest as social leader had already been established by Daniel O'Connell and his emancipation movement. Most pastors had behaved with heroic selflessness during the Famine, although a few abandoned their flocks, and in some cases their sense of priorities in the question of 'souperism' may have been inappropriate. They would be in the forefront of the constitutional struggle to settle the land question and the fight for what would come to be known as Home Rule.

One thing that the Famine had made clear was that Ireland was not, in practice, an integral part of the United Kingdom; the treatment shown it during the seven years of want was that of a colony – an entity that had connotations of exploitation for profit rather than partnership. As such novels as *Oliver Twist* and *Hard Times* indicate, the poor in Britain had a miserable time but did not starve. It was unthinkable that English or even Scottish citizens would have been allowed to perish in such numbers if the case had been altered. It was equally clear that a government in Dublin with control of internal finances would have handled relief more vigorously than Westminster and saved many lives. Although many of Mitchel's charges about the ratio of food imports were completely false – the rate of food imports was three times that of exports – his assertion that the British government could have done more to prevent the Famine is hard to challenge. The government's equal disregard of Irish landlords and Irish peasants, their comfortable sense that they were justified in their approach, their ruthless abrogation of financial responsibility at the height of the disaster, their hands-off attitude to 'the workings of economics' and their inaction during the 'exterminations' seemed in retrospect and to those in a position to observe at the time to be as close to criminal negligence as makes no difference.

Was it genocide, to use the modern word? Perhaps not. All the members of Russell's government wrung their hands in horror and both Peel and he made such strong verbal attacks on Irish landlords as to be actionable in other circumstances. But they did little else. The visitation was an appalling accident of nature and coping with it was beyond the capability of existing systems. But governments exist to deal with disasters as well as happier times. The trouble was that they did not really consider themselves the government of the intractable country and for that reason they failed her. The Union was terminally ill and the next seventy years were to produce the Famine harvest, to use a singularly inappropriate metaphor. Perhaps the attitude of such pious, churchgoing men as Trevelyan, Wood and the rest might be summed up in the words of Arthur Hugh Clough (1819–61) in his cynical verses 'The Latest Decalogue':

> *Thou shall not kill; but needst not strive*
> *Officiously to keep alive.*

One further piece of verse is tragically apposite. It is from *The Deserted Village*, which was written by Oliver Goldsmith (1728–74) in 1770 and is based the author's childhood memories of famine in Westmeath. It is eerily prophetic of the Ireland of three-quarters of a century later:

> *While scourged by famine from the smiling land*
> *The mournful peasant leads his humble band,*
> *And while he sinks, without one arm to save,*
> *The country blooms – a garden and a grave.*

# SELECT BIBLIOGRAPHY

Bardon, J. *A History of Ulster*. Belfast, 1992.

Boyce, G. and O'Day, A. (eds.) *The Making of Modern Irish History: Revisionism and the Revisionist Controversy*. London, 1996.

Brady, C. (ed.) *Interpreting Irish History*. Dublin, 1994.

D'Arcy, F. *The Story of Irish Emigration*. Dublin/Cork, 1999.

Eagleton, T. *Heathcliff and the Great Hunger: Studies in Irish Culture*. London, 1995.

Foster, R. *Modern Ireland 1600–1972*. London, 1990.

Gray, P. *Famine, Land and Politics*. Dublin, 1990.

Kee, R. *The Green Flag: Vol. I*. London, 1972.

Kinealy, C. *This Great Calamity: The Irish Famine*. Dublin, 1994.

Moody, T. W. and Martin, F. X. (eds.) *The Course of Irish History*. Cork, 1994.

Percival, J. *The Great Famine*. London, 1995.

Póirtéir, C. (ed.) *The Great Irish Famine*. Dublin/Cork, 1995.

Tóibín, C. *The Irish Famine*. London, 1999.

Vaughan, W. E. *A New History of Ireland: Vol. V*. Oxford, 1989.